THE GAY CLICHÉ

THE GAY CLICHÉ

Or
How to Be a
Homosexual Guy
and Still Maintain
Some Slight Degree
of Individuality

Tony Lang

Illustrations by Brett Woods

St. Martin's Press
New York

THE GAY CLICHÉ. Copyright © 1985 by Tony Lang and Brett Woods. All rights reserved. Printed in the United States of America. No part of this book may be used or reproduced in any manner whatsoever without written permission except in the case of brief quotations embodied in critical articles or reviews. For information, address St. Martin's Press, 175 Fifth Avenue, New York, N.Y. 10010.

Design by Deborah Daly

Library of Congress Cataloging in Publication Data

Lang, Tony.
   The gay cliché.
   1. Homosexuals, Male—Anecdotes, facetiae, satire, etc. 2. Individuality—Anecdotes, facetiae, satire, etc. I. Title.
HQ76.L36   1985   306.7'662   84-22268
ISBN 0-312-31793-X

First edition
10 9 8 7 6 5 4 3 2 1

For all the brave men
who have had the guts
and willpower not to
join a gym.

Contents

Introduction	8
General Appearance	11
Clothing	12
Grooming	16
The Gym	18
Other Exercise	21
Occupations	22
Love and Sex	25
A Few Notes on Pornography	28
The Classic Films	29
The Classic Stars	33
The Legitimate Stage	36
Music	38
The Dance	40
Television	42
Literature	44

Periodicals	46
Travel	48
Home Furnishings	53
Restaurants	58
A Few Notes on Brunch	59
Bars	60
Clubs	62
Pets	63
Friends	64
Psychoanalysis	65
A Note on Drugs	66
Fire Island	67
Family Relationships	68
Consciousness	72
A Note on the Word "Gay"	75
One Final Rule	77

INTRODUCTION

To some people, The Good Old Days refer to the time when you could buy two lamb chops without floating a loan. To others, it means that period during which it was possible to cross Washington Square Park at noon minus a police escort and a can of mace. There are, however, an ever-increasing number of those to whom The Good Old Days was that long-forgotten era when you could tell someone that you were a homosexual without having him fall asleep on you.

Progress—and I have a nagging suspicion that I may not be the first to have noticed this—is never a totally unmixed blessing. There's nothing for nothing, and all that. Our life span has become longer just as surely as our nerve endings have become shorter. And now that gay is becoming more and more Beautiful, there is a distinct possibility that it may also be becoming just the slightest bit Boring.

Now, we all need acceptance to a certain extent. There are very few of us who have the confidence and the stamina to stand stolidly alone against the mob. It is, however, possible to blend productively into the community without blending totally into the wallpaper. Keep in mind that history has given us a great many illustrious homosexuals and it is fairly safe to assume that most of them were a little bit—well, *different* from everybody else. It's doubtful, for instance, that when Michelangelo walked down the street, people turned to each other and said, "There goes another gay muralist. See? He's carrying his brushes on the left." In this age of creeping—if not galloping—conformity, why should the gay guy allow himself to be pigeonholed any more than is absolutely necessary?

And it is deceptively easy to unconsciously fall into certain styles and patterns. A quite innerly directed friend recently admitted to stopping in front of a mirror on Christopher Street to comb his hair only to come to the frightening realization that he had stopped not in front of a mirror but in front of a total stranger who looked exactly like himself. He has not worn a bomber jacket since.

It was this anecdote that suggested the writing of the pages that follow. It is to be hoped that they will be of some use. After all, this country of ours was built almost entirely on the concept of rugged individualism, and there is absolutely no reason that the gay guy shouldn't claim his heritage.

General Appearance

Don't shave your head.

Don't have a terrifically well-developed body unless you happen to be a professional middleweight.

Shave off all facial hair. The only acceptable possibilities are long, droopy Fu Manchu mustaches and stringy Vandyke goatees. Both of these looks, however, are so ugly that you would be wise to keep away from them. Remember, you are aiming for individuality, not alienation.

The above also holds true for ponytails.

Don't know the difference between delts, pecs and lats.

If you know the difference, don't do anything about it.

Your waist should not be smaller than 32 inches unless you are very short.

Try not to be very short.

Clothing

Don't wear anything made out of old parachutes.

Read *Gentlemen's Quarterly* regularly. Don't be caught dead in anything you see in it.

Unless you happen to be a burly Northwestern lumberjack, keep away from plaid shirts.

Don't buy clothes at boutiques with double entendre names.

Don't buy clothes at boutiques whose decor puts you in mind of World War II.

Don't buy clothes at boutiques. Buy them at hangarlike buildings located in suburban shopping malls.

It is sometimes all right to wear gym shorts, sweat socks and construction boots, but never all at once.

Wear a jockstrap only for athletic activity. If you have to wear one in the street, at least wear something over it.

If you are a motorcycle cop or a member of Hell's Angels, wear leather. If not, don't.

Either wear no earrings at all or wear two of them.

RECOMMENDED BASIC OUTFIT:

Loose-fitting, pleated gabardine pants; black shoes with laces; baggy, short-sleeved shirts with an inch or so of white T-shirt showing at the neck and three or four ballpoint pens showing at the pocket. I can't guarantee that you'll be the *only* gay person to be dressed this way, but the only other one I know of lives in Cleveland.

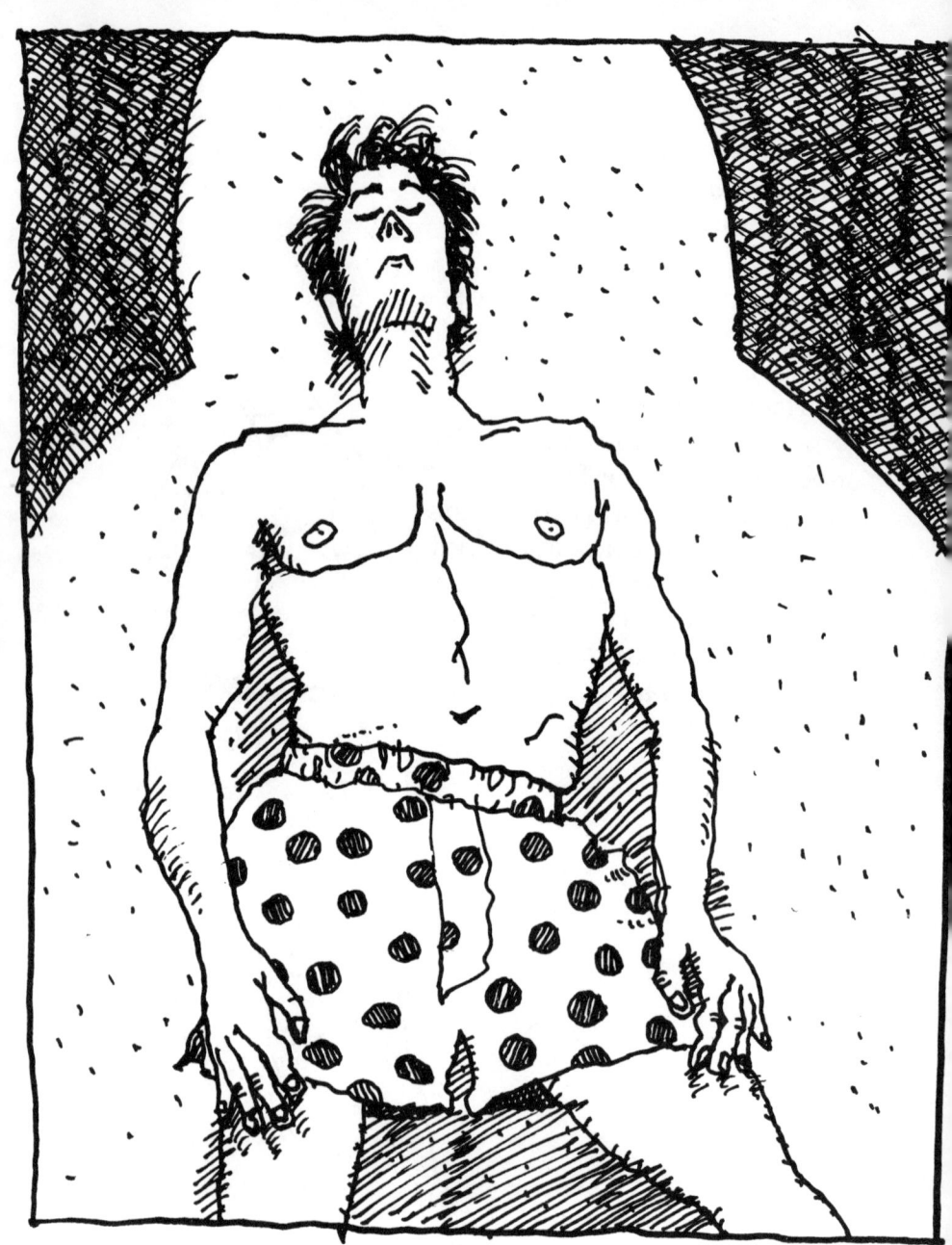

Wear boxer shorts. Score extra points if they're humorously illustrated with things like flames shooting out of the fly.

Wear sleeveless undershirts only under shirts. You may ignore this rule if you happen to be a middle-aged dockworker with a pot belly and a slatternly wife who wears grimy housedresses and drinks beer out of a can. However, there aren't all that many gay guys who meet these specifications.

Carry a bandanna only if you are a cleaning lady. If you do carry one, make sure its color and position mean absolutely nothing.

Use keys for opening doors. Don't wear them as jewelry.

Jogging shoes are technically okay, but give yourself extra points if you don't wear them.

Don't go barechested on the street unless you're drilling holes in it.

Keep away from briefs. If you have to wear them, make sure they're at least brief and not non-existent.

Hooded sweat shirts are iffy.

But bomber jackets are definitely out.

Scarves are *very* dangerous.

Grooming

Try not to use a hair dryer.

Don't use soap that comes on ropes.

Don't have a shelf system in your shower that would be capable of handling half of the cosmetic stock at Bloomingdale's.

Don't have a ten-speed shower nozzle. If your nozzle is equipped to do more things to your body than your lover is, get rid of it.

Do not wear cologne unless it's Old Spice. There are no alternatives.

Don't use designer label shampoo. Stick to one of those generic brands that cost ninety-eight cents a half gallon.

Chapstick is probably okay, but you'd be better off without it.

Don't get haircuts that cost over $150. And don't get all that chummy with the guy who does it for you. You may inquire after his health, but don't compare diseases. Actually, there are still a few elderly men around who cut hair for $2.50 and don't speak English. Try to find one of them.

Don't augment a tan with anything from a bottle.

Don't be tan unless you live in California.

Don't live in California.

GENERAL COSMETIC RULE: If you can picture Lauren Hutton using it, don't.

The Gym

Avoid it like the plague. If, however, you are one of those unfortunate souls who have already built an entire life around it, at least heed the following rules:

Don't arrive by taxi.

Don't do warm-up exercises that look as if they've been choreographed by Twyla Tharp.

Don't bring your personal brand of soap into the shower room—especially Pear's.

If a straight guy happens to wander into your gym, don't flash him a big grin and try to relate to him on his own terms.

Don't talk about:
    a) the Saint.
    b) the Pines.
    c) "Dynasty."

While exercising, do not wear:
  a) Painter's caps—especially turned backward.
  b) Tank tops that read:
     1. UCLA.
     2. Maui.
     3. U.S. Marine Corps.
     4. Pittsburgh Steelers Training Camp.
  c) Any shirt casually ripped to expose one or more nipples.
  d) Gray wool socks with shocking pink top bands.
  e) Black Adidas.

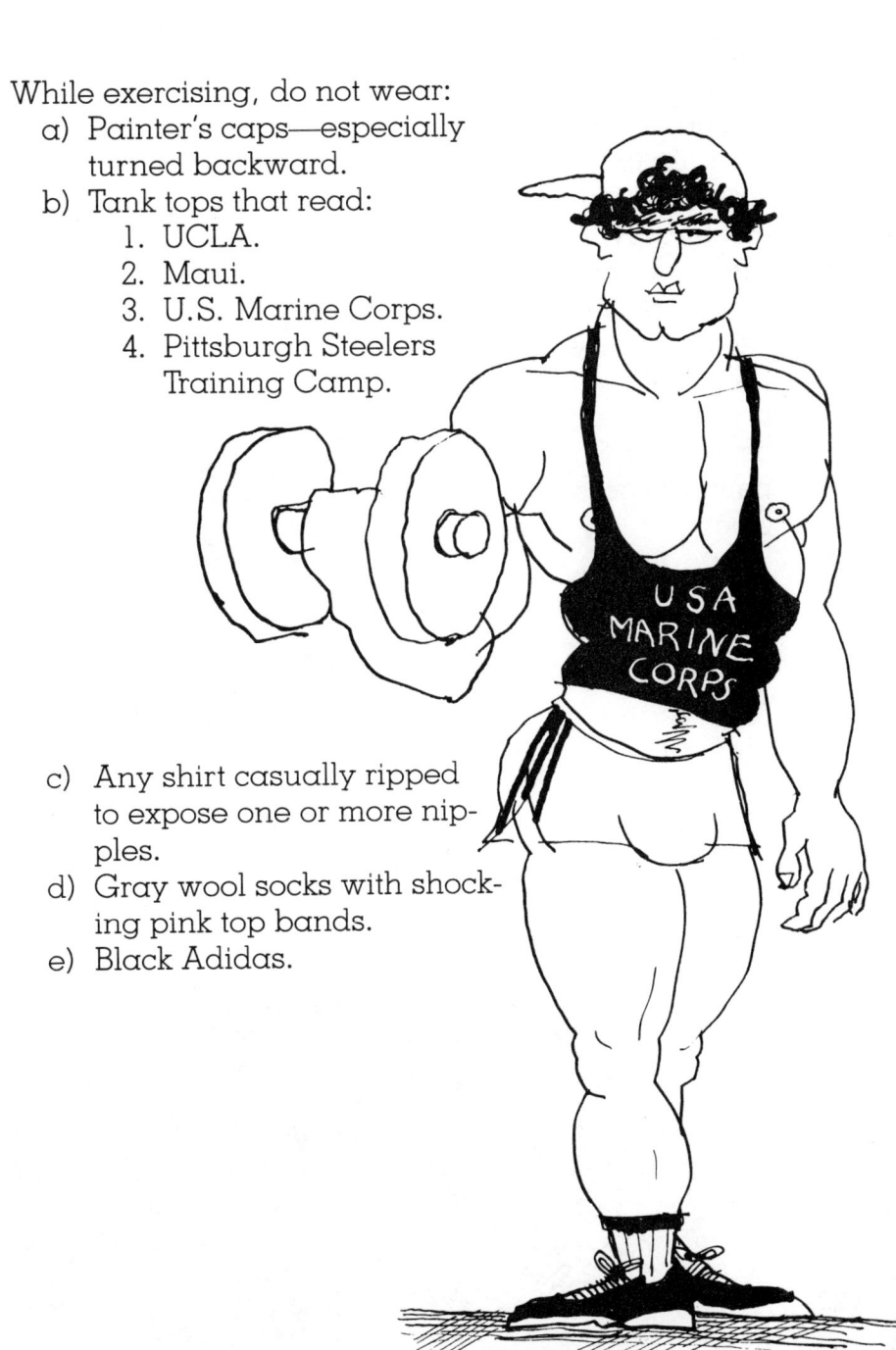

RECOMMENDED BASIC GYM OUTFIT: Spotlessly clean white V-neck T-shirt one size too large; Bermuda shorts (preferably madras) with underwear showing above the waist and/or below the knee; brand-new navy blue basketball sneakers with black lisle socks. Score extra points if socks have clocks.

Other Exercise

Don't roller skate. Especially, don't roller skate in a dress.

Jogging is technically okay, but give yourself extra points if you don't do it.

The Frisbee craze seems to be pretty much over. Don't bring it back.

Try not to dance at all, but definitely don't dance:
    a) with a tambourine
    b) with amyl nitrite
    c) during sex

Occupations

Don't be an attendant at the baths.

Don't do part-time market research.

Don't write for small film quarterlies.

It's all right to be in window display as long as you work in one of those hangarlike stores located in suburban shopping malls. Any place else is out.

It's all right to be a copywriter as long as you're not at work on a novel.

It's all right to be at work on a novel as long as it's not about growing up gay in small towns in the South.

Be any kind of an athlete except an ice skater—especially one who turns pro and joins the Ice Capades.

Don't be a dress designer.
Be a garment manufacturer.

Don't be an actor unless you're making at least $100,000 a year or are Paul Newman, whichever comes first.

Don't be a nurse.

It's okay to be a painter.
But not an illustrator.

Similarly, it's okay to be a poet.
But not a lyricist.

Don't own a health-food restaurant.
Own a delicatessen.

Be president of the United States.

Don't be the pope.

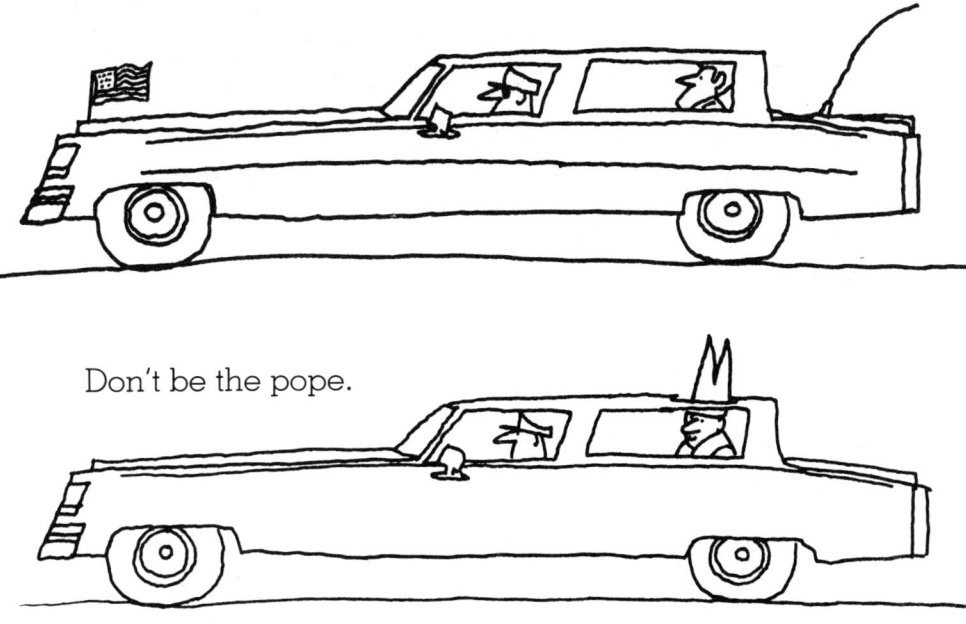

BIGGEST OCCUPATIONAL UPSET OF THE DECADE: It is suddenly all right to be a hairdresser. No one really knows how this happened.

But being an interior decorator is still out. If you call yourself an interior designer, it's further out. Which brings us to:

THE NEWEST OCCUPATIONAL TABOO: Don't be a landscape architect. It would be nice to report that it's still all right to be a gardener, but it's not—unless you're an elderly man who doesn't speak English and charges $2.50. Once again, there aren't too many gay guys who fit this description—especially the $2.50 part.

Love and Sex

Know the first and last names of the person you have most recently slept with.

If you are going steady with someone, have sex with other people only two or three times a week.

If you are truly in love, have sex with other people only once or twice a month.

Don't be truly in love more than two or three times a year.

Orgies are okay, but there don't seem to be too many being given these days. Strangely enough, there are a *lot* of them in Cleveland. I do not really think, however, that this fact makes moving there worthwhile.

Don't be 100 percent certain about the differences between a Trick, a Number, a Thing, a Relationship and a Lover. Get them confused once in a while. Try occasionally to have a Thing with a Lover or a Relationship with a Trick.

If you are having a tragic love affair, don't call the Gay Switchboard for advice.

Don't have tragic love affairs.

THE ACID TEST:
   a) You meet someone terrific who thinks you're terrific and you can't keep your hands off each other.
   b) You don't sleep with each other until the following night.
   (I do not personally know of anyone—gay *or* straight—who has ever managed to pull this off. Be the first.)

TWO RULES FOR BISEXUAL MEN:
1. Have had sex with a woman at least twice in your life.
2. Have enjoyed it at least once.

When ending a love affair, don't say:

   a) "I guess I'm not ready for a permanent relationship."
   b) "It's not you, it's me."
   c) "Can't we be friends?"

A Few Notes on Pornography

Don't go around saying how boring you find it. On the other hand, don't get too involved. If you can name the person who did the incidental music for *Boys in the Sand,* you've gone over the edge.

Don't go to porno theaters with a friend and giggle.

Go by yourself and masturbate.

Watch pornography with your lover as long as it's an addition to—not a substitute for—your relationship.

It's all right to admire Jack Wrangler, but try not to know him personally. This, I must warn you, becomes more difficult all the time.

The Classic Films

All About Eve. Never even *mention* this one. If it happens to come up in conversation, just say that you enjoyed it and try to change the subject. When asked how many times you have seen it, say, "Once." And don't *ever* quote a line from it. If anyone else does, smile distractedly as if you don't know what the hell they're talking about. Do not, however, go to extremes and say that you hated this picture. There really isn't anyone who *didn't* like it, and you don't want to be suspected of protesting too much.

Whatever Happened to Baby Jane? Like it, but like it as a horror movie, not as a comedy. And don't sing along with "I've Written a Letter to Daddy."

Meet Me in St. Louis. This is one of the few safe Judy Garland movies, so feel free to be enthusiastic about it. You can even say that you cried when Judy sang "Have Yourself a Merry Little Christmas" to Margaret O'Brien. Do not, however, know the verse of "The Trolley Song" or remember the names of any of the other players. Especially Lucille Bremer.

Dark Victory. Think that this was the movie in which Paul Henried lit two cigarettes.

Now Voyager. Think that this was the movie in which Bette Davis went blind.

Gone with the Wind. Think whatever you like about it, but don't do imitations of Butterfly McQueen.

Singin' in the Rain. Ditto Jean Hagen.

Imitation of Life. (the Lana Turner version). Don't think that this is the funniest movie ever made. Just think it's stupid.

The Boys in the Band. Don't take a particularly strong position on this one. Don't love it and don't hate it. Ideally, don't ever have seen it.

A Star Is Born. Don't claim that the Janet Gaynor-Fredric March original was the best. (In fact, don't even *know* about the Gaynor-March version.) And since this next sentence is perhaps the key one in this whole book, I'm giving it a page all to itself:

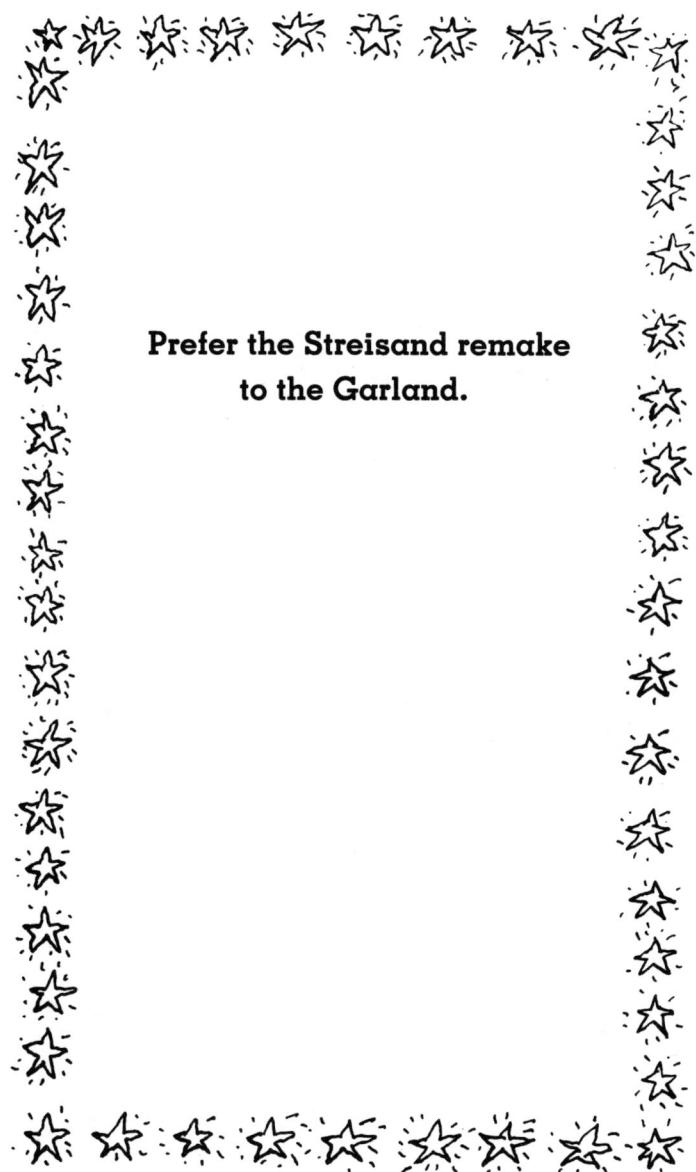

Prefer the Streisand remake to the Garland.

This may at times put you in actual physical danger, but being an individual was never easy.

The Classic Stars

It's finally safe to like Barbra Streisand. But *like* her, don't be *insane* about her. (Don't be *insane* about *anybody*.)

Don't like Judy Garland but don't really hate her, either. When asked about her say, "She's okay, I guess."

Really hate Bette Davis.

It's always been hard to have a definitive rule about Liza Minnelli. At the moment that this is being written, she's all right. This situation, however, could change any minute. Use your own judgment. To play it really safe, keep away from her altogether.

Like Doris Day—but not to the extent of thinking that she's the most underrated actress Hollywood has ever produced.

You don't have to hate Mae West, but be very careful with her. And don't think she's a man in drag.

And don't have any inside dish on the Rock Hudson/Jim Nabors business.

Love John Wayne to death.

Don't make fun of Elizabeth Taylor's taste. And don't know the names of her ex-husbands in chronological order.

Also, don't know the names of Ann Blyth's studios in chronological order. I realize that this may sound like a rather baroque rule, but since I know of at least two people who can do just that, it may not be as baroque as we hope.

Love the Marx Brothers. Even better, love the Ritz Brothers. But leave the Andrews Sisters alone.

Katharine Hepburn is another tough one. See Liza Minnelli.

It's perfectly safe to like Woody Allen but, just for the hell of it, don't.

Don't be terribly impressed by John Travolta's new body.

And don't find Ann Miller all that amusing.

A NOTE ON MOVIE THEATERS

Keep out of intimate revival houses—especially those that show double bills of *Dinner at Eight* and *The Women.*

The Legitimate Stage

Avoid it as much as is humanly possible.

It is now all right to like Tennessee Williams. Do not, however, get into things like the Tallulah Bankhead revival of *The Milk Train Doesn't Stop Here Anymore*.

Like Arthur Miller much more than Tennessee Williams, and don't think *After the Fall* was self-indulgent.

Don't be condescending about Neil Simon.

And don't hate Edward Albee. The critics have finally done it for you.

Think that Sam Shepard, Lanford Wilson and David Mamet are the same person.

THREE STEPHEN SONDHEIM RULES:

    1. Don't get into discussions about how *Company* was his last good show and how he has become too inbred and arty for words.
    2. Don't have a theory about how *Merrily We Roll Along* could have worked. And don't love the cast album. Don't even know that it was recorded.
    3. Absolutely loathe *Sweeney Todd*.

Don't go to previews of disasters that are obviously going to close before they open. If you do, don't have a terrific time.

And speaking of which, don't be one of the people who saw *Moose Murders*. Definitely don't be someone who saw it before Eve Arden quit.

Like *Gypsy* but don't start comparing the Ethel Merman original and the Angela Lansbury revival.

In general, though, it's okay to like Ethel Merman.

But not Angela Lansbury—especially in *Sweeney Todd*.

Don't do a whole number on Chita Rivera's professionalism.

Don't make fun of Sandy Dennis.
But don't like her, either.

Love George C. Scott no matter what he does—including plays in which he appears with his wife.

Like his wife.

It's also all right to like Alan Jay Lerner's wife, but it's not all right to know who she is. I wish I could be more helpful on this, but I don't make the rules.

Don't be bitchy about Lauren Bacall.

Leave *Torch Song Trilogy, La Cage Aux Folles* and Harvey Fierstein alone. If this is impossible (which it just about is), hate them all.

Don't wonder what happened to Zohra Lampert.

Music

Don't know *anything* about opera. Especially, don't know about sopranos and their fatal flaws. If you have to have an opera record, make it something like Robert Merrill and Rïse Stevens singing selections from *The Merry Widow*.

Don't know who Anna Russell is. If you do, don't have committed her analysis of the "Ring" cycle to memory. If you have, don't quote lines from it. If you do, don't quote, "I'm not making this up, you know." If you have any idea of what I'm talking about, you're in trouble.

Have some records of folk songs that deal with the labor movement.

Hate *all* disco music. There is no exception to this rule.

Prefer Rodgers and Hammerstein to Rodgers and Hart. Rodgers and Hart songs are safe only if they have been recorded by Frank Sinatra.

Love Frank Sinatra. Also like Tony Bennett, Vic Damone, Perry Como, Jerry Vale, Connie Francis and that whole crowd. Have a whole bunch of their records on which they sing "Italian Favorites."

Don't like Johnny Mathis unless you really know what you're doing.

Like jazz but don't be *too* crazy about Billie Holiday. Play Modern Jazz Quartet albums. (If you really have guts, play Dave Brubeck.)

Love Harry Belafonte.

But love Sammy Davis, Jr., even more. Be *extremely* fond of him. Be warned, however: **This is almost as dangerous as loving the Streisand *Star is Born*.**

Don't like Barbara Cook. Don't even be sure who she is. This goes double for Julie Wilson.

Have the Original Cast Albums of:
   a) *Hair*
   b) *The Wiz*
   c) *Grease*

Do *not* have the Original Cast Albums of:
   a) *Hazel Flagg*
   b) *Whoop-Up*
   c) *Flahooley*

The Dance

It's all right to say that you like ballet. Just don't ever go to it.

Try to calmly accept the fact that Baryshnikov is straight. Don't take an overdose every time you see him photographed with a woman.

And try to watch *The Turning Point* as comedy-drama, not as soft-core porn.

Don't think Makarova is the funniest woman ever born.

Prefer Gene Kelly to Fred Astaire, but don't be able to name too many of his films—especially *The Pirate*.

Don't bemoan the fact that Ann Reinking's career has never really taken off.

Don't know anyone who has had sex with Nureyev.

Don't have had sex with Nureyev.

SECOND BIGGEST OCCUPATIONAL UPSET OF THE DECADE: It is suddenly all right to be a dancer. Now, I know how *this* happened—*A Chorus Line* did it. Speaking of which, it's all right to like *A Chorus Line* as long as you don't understand what they're talking about. And don't have been there for its record-breaking performance for which they got together everyone who had ever been in the thing. If you were there, don't think it was the most moving experience of your life. Think it was a big waste of half a million bucks.

Television

Watch only prime-time programming—except "Dynasty."

Don't watch anything on Public Broadcasting. Especially:
- a) 80-hour adaptations of obscure English novels
- b) Anything taped at the Kennedy Center
- c) Twyla Tharp

Like David Susskind. Actually, it was a lot classier to like Susskind in the days when he thought that homosexuality was a major disease. But like him anyway. You'll still be in a very elite minority.

Watch the Miss America Pageant and manage to keep a straight face during the entire talent section.

Watch the Jerry Lewis Labor Day Telethon. Think that he is sincere.

It's okay to watch hockey as long as you enjoy it as a sport and not as a sadomasochistic fantasy. If you find yourself getting an erection during a Rangers game, you are not taking it in the right spirit.

Reruns of "The Mary Tyler Moore Show" are fine, but try not to get too carried away by Betty White.

Reruns of "The Honeymooners" are also okay as long as your favorite episode isn't "Alice Gets the Apartment Redecorated" and your favorite character isn't Trixie.

BASIC RULES FOR WATCHING THE ACADEMY AWARDS:

1. Don't watch it in large groups.
2. Don't make fun of the gowns.
3. Don't make fun of the hairdos.
4. Don't make fun of Jane Fonda.

BASIC RULES FOR WATCHING THE TONY AWARDS:

1. Don't watch it in large groups.
2. Don't think that this year's show is the absolute worst to date.
3. Don't make snide comments about Hildy Parks. If anyone else does say, "Who's she?"
4. Don't totally crack up when a guy thanks his male lover. This may seem like another baroque rule, but I sense a trend.
5. Don't say that you are never going to watch the Tony Awards again.
6. Never watch the Tony Awards again.

BASIC RULES FOR WATCHING THE SUPER BOWL:

1. Know what it is.
2. Watch it.

Literature

Don't read biographies of movie stars—especially female movie stars. Most especially Shelley Winters. It is, however, okay to *like* Shelley Winters. Once again, this is something that I can't really explain.

Don't read books that reveal the inside dope about Broadway musicals.

Norman Mailer is okay except when he writes about Marilyn Monroe.

Surprisingly enough, it's all right to read Oscar Wilde. You would think that this would make Noel Coward okay, but it doesn't.

Somerset Maugham is a problem.

It's all right to read Thurber, S. J. Perelman, Ring Lardner, Damon Runyon, Art Buchwald and even Jean Kerr. Actually, it seems that just about all humorists are safe.

Except Fran Lebowitz. If you do read her, don't understand most of it—especially her references to Ronald Firbank.

Be totally ignorant of Ronald Firbank.

Don't read Ernest Hemingway. It's not that he isn't okay—if anything, he's a little *too* okay. Liking him is sort of like not liking *All About Eve.*

It's all right to read Philip Roth, John Updike, Saul Bellow and John Cheever. In fact, it's okay to read just about any modern American novel except those about growing up gay in small towns in the South.

English novels, however, are a whole other story—especially those written by women. Be very careful with Muriel Spark and Iris Murdoch. More so with Ivy Compton-Burnett. And read Jane Austen only if you're extremely secure. See Johnny Mathis.

Read any mystery except those written by Carleton Carpenter. If you didn't know that Carleton Carpenter wrote mysteries, you're ahead. If you don't know who Carleton Carpenter *is*, you're *way* ahead.

Periodicals

Buy the Sunday *Times*. Then:
   1. Throw out the Arts and Leisure section and the Book Review.
   2. Keep the Sports and Business sections. For extra points, actually read the news.
   3. Keep the Magazine. But:
      a) Don't read the food, fashion or home design articles.
      b) Read those articles with such titles as:
         1. "A Return to Yugoslavia."
         2. "The Suburban Roots of the New Federalism."
         3. "India's Forced March to Modernity."
      c) Don't do the crossword puzzle. You may, however, do the Puns and Anagrams. Don't ask me why.

Don't read *New York* magazine. But if—like those people who go to the gym—you find that it's too late to stop, at least:
   a) Read and (this is the important part) *like* John Simon. Liking John Simon is even better than liking David Susskind.
   b) Don't read—and definitely don't *enter*—the Competition. You will realize the importance of this rule when I tell you that Carleton Carpenter is a frequent contributor.

It's probably all right to read *The New Yorker*, but my gut instinct says no.

Read *Playboy.*

But don't read *Popular Mechanics.* See Ernest Hemingway.

You can read *The Advocate, Christopher Street, Blueboy,* et al, but only for the personal ads. And I don't mean for their camp value—you have to *answer* them. The basic rules here are:
    1. Don't answer ads placed by people who are looking for nature-loving nonsmokers.
    2. Answer ads placed by people who are looking for filthy sex.
    3. Never run an ad yourself. Those who do are, without exception, lethally unattractive.

Travel

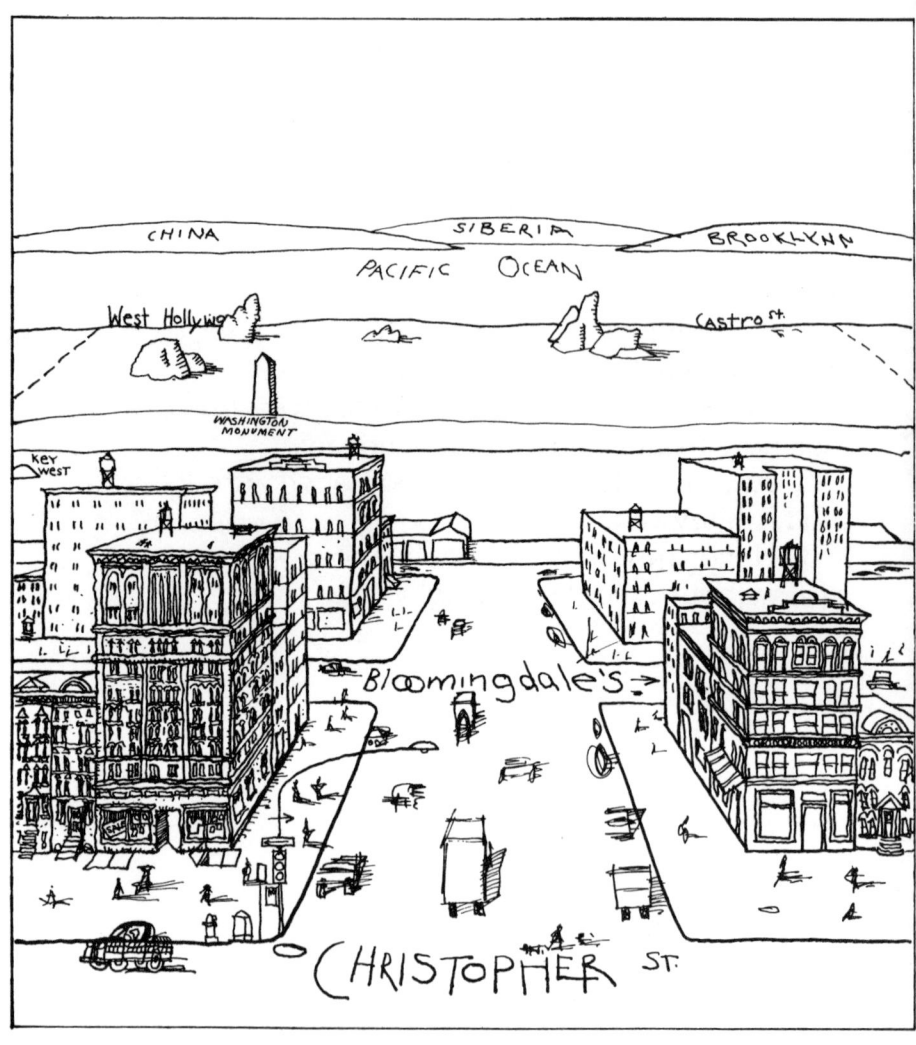

Key West is to towns as gyms are to exercise. Keep very far away from it. Don't even know where it is. Think it's in Cuba.

Cuba's okay.

But not Puerto Rico—especially if you stay at one of those sympatico guesthouses that only three people in the world know about. Go to Puerto Rico only if you are Puerto Rican.

Hawaii is sort of up for grabs. But keep in mind the fact that Bette Midler was raised there.

It's all right to visit New Jersey (if you can possibly find a reason to do so), but don't live there.

New Orleans is almost as bad as Key West.

Keep away from London. Paris is okay, and Madrid is even better. Better still is almost *any* city in Ireland.

All of the Scandinavian countries are suspect—especially Denmark.

Mararakesh used to be really off limits. It may be all right by now, but why take a chance?

China is safe. India is even safer. Israel is *very* safe, but it's even less fun than China and India (if such a thing is possible).

This one is so obvious that it should either not be mentioned at all or be given a double-page spread. Since I happen to be the nervous type, I'll opt for the latter . . .

Don't Go To

San Francisco!!!

(If you happen to be there now, leave. Don't even finish this book.)

A Note on Luggage

Don't carry anything made out of old parachutes.

Home Furnishings

Keep away from plants. If you absolutely must, have a pot of geraniums and let it go at that. Try not to have a living room in which Tarzan would feel at home.

And if you happen to find yourself with a leftover avocado pit, throw it out. Don't wait to see what it grows up to be.

Stick to white sheets. Especially avoid brown geometric prints.

Also avoid having brown walls. (Brown seems generally to be pretty dangerous.)

Don't have shower curtains that come in layers.

Have light switches that turn on and off, and nothing else. Don't have a dimmer system that would be capable of lighting a full-scale production of *Dreamgirls*.

Do not be able to even *define* art deco.

If you have pictures of naked men, keep them in a drawer as a sex aid, don't hang them on the walls as art.

Don't have a big glass coffee table.

Don't have a coffee table that was something else in another life.

Score extra points if you don't have a coffee table.

Don't go in for the "country" look—especially ruffles.

Lofts can go either way. See hooded sweat shirts.

It's all right to have industrial carpeting and track lighting if your apartment happens to double as the reception room of a small ad agency. If it doesn't, don't.

Do not own copper fish molds, trivets or cloth napkins. I trust I don't even have to mention napkin rings.

Don't own a pepper mill. And salt shakers should be simple things with holes on the top. They should not require an operating manual.

For cooking, use a pot, a frying pan and not much else. Do not get into the type of utensil that even Julia Child would refer to as "optional."

You would think that Tiffany lamps would finally be okay, but they aren't.

Avoid Moroccan-type draped fabrics, beaded curtains, etc. Don't have a bedroom in which Yvonne de Carlo would feel at home.

Don't have mirrors in places in which they are obviously up to no good.

Restaurants

Don't go to those at which you have dated more than one of the waiters.

Try to avoid those little storefront operations that serve overpriced French food and seat less than six people.

Don't go to restaurants that have waiters in black tie serving customers in rags.

Avoid places that try to approximate the ambience of early Warner Brothers movies—especially *Casablanca*.

Sardi's is all right as long as you're not blasé about the celebs. If you see George C. Scott, stare at him. If you see Chita Rivera, however, don't recognize her.

When eating out, try to order:
    a) Pot roast
    b) Pork chops
    c) Fish cakes and spaghetti

Try *not* to order:
    a) Chicken Cordon Bleu
    b) Anything Florentine
    c) Anything *con prosciutto*—especially *melone*.

Eat quiche. (Fuck 'em.)

But don't eat brunch. Speaking of which . . .

A Few Notes on Brunch: Brunch is to meals as Key West is to towns. If you absolutely must get involved with one, at least call it a late breakfast. (This may strain credulity a bit, since most brunches seem to get going at an hour that is more appropriate to an early dinner.)

Don't go to brunches that are predominantly male but include one or two jolly middle-aged women to whom everyone is very polite but for whom they are secretly waiting to leave so that they can really talk.

Don't go to brunches that are large enough to require the services of a bartender. Particularly a very young, pretty one whom everyone is continually and unsuccessfully trying to make.

Don't drink combinations of champagne and orange juice.

(I could go on, but my heart isn't really in it. Once you find youself at a brunch, the damage is pretty much done, so you may as well just relax and enjoy yourself. This, unfortunately, is almost always impossible.)

Bars

Don't go to theater-type hangouts—especially those that feature posters of flop shows.

Keep out of bars in which the customers look like the supporting cast of *The Wild One*. If you wind up in one, don't lean up against the wall looking mean and not talking to anybody. Go up to the person who is wearing the most frightening-looking outfit, flash him a big smile and say, "Hey, you're not really *serious*, are you?" (Then run.)

Bars that have TV are almost always okay—but be careful. If they start showing tapes of old Tony Award shows, get the hell out.

Go to Irish bars that have little rooms in the back reserved for "ladies and their escorts." Stay out of any other kind of bar with little rooms in the back.

Don't go to piano bars where young, unemployed actors get up and sing. Definitely don't *be* a young, unemployed actor who gets up and sings. Actually, the only safe piano bars are those found in run-down midtown hotels in which fading blond ladies play and drunken out-of-town businessmen sing along. If you find yourself in one of these, it's all right to request songs and even to sing along to the following:
    a) "As Time Goes By"
    b) "What Kind of Fool Am I?"
    c) "My Way"
Do *not* request:
    a) "You Could Drive a Person Crazy"
    b) "You Gotta Have a Gimmick"
    c) "Guess Who I Saw Today, My Dear"
Problem song:
        "Tomorrow"

Clubs

Don't go to those that try to approximate the ambience of old RKP movies—especially *The Gay Divorcee.*

Don't go to clubs that reserve Monday nights for new talent.

Don't be a new talent.

Don't go to clubs at which ladies who haven't been on Broadway for a while are doing two weeks. Gretchen Wyler is a good example.

Frances Faye and Kay Thompson don't seem to be around much these days. This has made life a lot easier.

Bobby Short, however, is everywhere. Try to avoid him.

But it's all right to go to see Arthur Siegel. Actually, it isn't *that* all right, but Arthur is a friend and needs all the help he can get. By the way, if you know who Arthur Siegel is, you're *really* in trouble.

Pets

Don't have an Afghan.

It's okay to have a poodle as long as you keep it more or less in its natural state. When it starts looking more affluent than you do, you've gone too far.

Don't name your pet after anyone who has sung at the Met—especially Renata Tebaldi.

It's all right to have a parakeet, but don't teach it to say things like "Fasten your seatbelts."

Don't get into an overly intimate relationship with your cat.

Don't get drunk and dress your cat in drag.

Don't have a cat.

Have a turtle.

Friends

If you are at a bar with a friend, look at him at least as often as you do at the door.

Don't call a friend a sister unless:
    a) she is a woman and
    b) you share at least one parent in common.

Don't have friends who are continually trying to commit suicide.

RULES ABOUT GIRL FRIENDS:
    1. Don't have girl friends who know a lot of show tunes.
    2. Don't have a girl friend who is always trying to get you into bed unless you occasionally let her get you into bed.
    3. Don't have a girl friend who is Sylvia Miles.

Don't have a friend who reads Rex Reed.

Don't have a friend who *is* Rex Reed.

Don't have been a friend of Bette Midler's when she was a struggling chorus singer just off the boat from Hawaii.

Be a friend of hers now.

If you're not a friend of Bette Midler's, don't get to know any other chunky, campy girls with great voices. That trend is pretty much over and it is doubtful that she will ever make it.

Don't have friends from New Jersey.

Psychoanalysis

Try going straight. Some Liberation types may attempt to beat you up, but you will certainly stand out from the crowd. I know of only one guy who has tried to go straight in the past ten years and he lives in Cleveland. Of course, no gay shrink will be a party to this, but that's all right—especially taking into account the following rule:

Don't have a gay shrink.

Or, for that matter, a gay M.D.

Have a gay dentist.

A Note on Drugs

Moderation is the word here. On the one hand, you don't want to be one of those people who run around saying, "I don't even take aspirin" (this type is invariably a real pain in the ass). On the other, do not be a pharmacological encyclopedia. This is a person who takes no less than six different controlled substances in order to enjoy half an hour on Fire Island and can tell you in elaborate detail which pill most enhances a viewing of *Superman III*.

And speaking of Fire Island . . .

Fire Island

Don't share a house with more than eight people, and don't wind up hating more than six of them.

Don't lie on the beach and make fun of the straights.

Eat dinner before dawn.

But don't eat tuna-and-noddle casseroles.

Don't get into fights about laundry—especially bath towels.

Don't get into fights about food—especially cold cuts.

Don't plant anything—especially parsley.

Don't invite a straight girl out for the weekend and watch her get suicidally depressed.

Go out with your lover.

Stay with him.

Family Relationships

When your parents ask you why you're not married, don't say:

"Mom, Pop, there's something I have to tell you. I'm gay. I've always been gay and I just don't want to hide it anymore. I'm tired of living a lie. I hope you'll understand and that we can be a whole lot closer from now on. I'd like you to meet Sheldon."

Say:

"Married?! Are you nuts? With the stable of chicks *I've* built up? And I'm not talking dogs, I'm talking Class-A stuff. By the way, this is Shelly. He gets my leftovers, ha-ha."

Consciousness

WHEN ON MARCHES:

1. Don't make campy remarks to the cops.
2. Don't yell things in unison.
3. Dress appropriately. If the march takes place in the afternoon, don't wear an evening gown.

4. Don't make derisive remarks about the lesbians who are marching with you.

5. Don't make derisive remarks about the gay men who are marching with you.

6. Don't cruise.

WHEN AT GAY CHURCHES OR SYNAGOGUES:

1. Pray.
2. Don't cruise.

WHEN AT DISCUSSION GROUPS:

1. Don't talk about the difficulty you are having in accepting your sexuality.
2. Don't talk about the success you are having in accepting your sexuality.
3. Don't use the word *identity*.
4. Don't talk about how difficult it is to relate at the bars.
5. Don't talk about how difficult it is to relate at the baths.
6. Don't use the word *relate*.
7. Don't cruise.
8. Don't go to discussion groups.

A Note on the Word "Gay"

Don't use it.*

---

* I regret to say that this is next to impossible. As you have doubtless noticed, even I (who, of all people, should be setting a good example) have

not been able to get around it. Even in the *title*.

I realize that there was a relatively recent period—before "gay" had completely inundated the world of sit-com—when people went around not saying it all the time. The trouble is, no one seems to remember quite how this was swung. I suppose *homosexual* was used a lot, and it is still a perfectly respectable and certainly accurate word. At this point, however, it seems terribly academic and pedantic. (You don't want to start sounding like one of those people who insist on calling every female over the age of two weeks a "woman.") Which leaves you with words like *queer, fag* and *fruit.* Now, these are perfectly fine to use among sophisticated friends. Unfortunately, not everyone is all that sophisticated or friendly (especially in Cleveland). Someone might very easily try to kill you, and there is no real point to being an individual if you're going to be a dead one.

One Final Rule

Don't follow every rule in this book.

I realize that this may sound just a bit contradictory and, perhaps, even self-defeating. But if it turns out that you have scored 100 percent, you are probably either:

a) a fanatic or

b) a middle-aged dockworker with a pot belly and a slatternly wife who wears grimy housedresses and drinks beer out of a can.

I have already noted the unlikelihood of the latter possibility, and nobody loves a fanatic. They may be quite admirable people, but they are in general not all that much fun to hang around with. Joan of Arc is a good example.

Now, I am certainly not suggesting that you set my advice at naught, only that you don't go overboard in either direction (see Drugs and Judy Garland). And once you have caught the spirit of the thing, you need not stick unyieldingly to the letter. Example: The other day I ran into a friend (whom I personally regard as being individual almost to the point of being weird) who was wearing a bomber jacket *over* a hooded sweatshirt *over* a plaid shirt. Now, ordinarily, this would have been grounds for ending the friendship. But it was the *way* he wore this X-rated outfit that made the difference. Even the sardonic curl of his lip seemed to say, "I know what you're thinking and it doesn't faze me in the least. *I* can get away with this and we both know it. *You*, on the other hand, had better not even try." (The curl of my friend's lip can speak volumes.) And, I'm afraid to say, he was right on the money.

So let's just deal with all of the preceding rules as casually as possible. If any of the above is going to take, the process is already at work. And if not—well, there's no point in agonizing over it. Just relax and have a nice brunch.